Mat...

The Silver Linings Playbook

BOOKCAPS

A BookCaps™ Study Guide

www.bookcaps.com

© 2012. All Rights Reserved.

Table of Contents

ABOUT BOOKCAPS 5

HISTORICAL CONTEXT 6

PLOT OVERVIEW 9

THEMES 12

    SEEING THE "SILVER LINING" 12
    BEING KIND INSTEAD OF RIGHT 13
    IMPORTANCE OF FRIENDSHIP AND ACCEPTANCE 14
    MENTAL INSTABILITY 15
    DENIAL 16
    DOMESTIC DISPUTES 17
    LITERATURE AS A REFLECTION OF PEOPLE 17
    MOVIES AND VISUAL PICTURES 18
    SPORTS AND PHYSICAL ACTIVITY 19
    TRANSFORMATION 19

CHARACTERS 21

    PAT PEOPLES 21
    TIFFANY 22
    NIKKI 22
    CLIFF (DR. PATEL) 23
    MOM 24
    DAD 24
    JAKE 25
    RONNIE 25
    VERONICA 26
    EMILY 26
    CAITLIN 27
    SCOTT 27
    DANNY 28
    DR. TIMBERS 28
    HANK BASKETT 29

CHAPTER SUMMARY 30

    CHAPTER 1: AN INFINITE AMOUNT OF DAYS UNTIL MY INEVITABLE REUNION WITH NIKKI 31

CHAPTER 2: HE DOES NOT PREACH PESSIMISM 33
CHAPTER 3: ORANGE FIRE ENTERS MY SKULL 36
CHAPTER 4: THE WORST ENDING IMAGINABLE.....................37
CHAPTER 5: GOT NOTHIN' BUT LOVE FOR YA......................38
CHAPTER 6: THE CONCRETE DOUGHNUT 39
CHAPTER 7: I FEAR HIM MORE THAN ANY OTHER BEING 40
CHAPTER 8: THE DRESS-UP DINNER 41
CHAPTER 9: IF I BACKSLIDE 42
CHAPTER 10: I DON'T KNOW HOW THIS WORKS 43
CHAPTER 11: FILLED WITH MOLTEN LAVA 45
CHAPTER 12: FAILING LIKE DIMMESDALE DID.....................46
CHAPTER 13: DO YOU LIKE FOREIGN FILMS? 47
CHAPTER 14: I CAN SHARE RAISIN BRAN..............................48
CHAPTER 15: SING AND SPELL AND CHANT..........................49
CHAPTER 16: THE BEST THERAPIST IN THE ENTIRE WORLD .51
CHAPTER 17: TIFFANY'S HEAD FLOATING OVER THE WAVES
....52
CHAPTER 18: A HIVE FULL OF GREEN BEES..........................54
CHAPTER 19: SISTER SAILOR MOUTH....................................56
CHAPTER 20: THE IMPLIED ENDING.......................................57
CHAPTER 21: AN ACCEPTABLE FORM OF COPING 58
CHAPTER 22: BALANCED VERY CAREFULLY, AS IF THE
WHOLE THING MIGHT TOPPLE WHEN THE HEATER VENTS
BEGIN TO BLOW LATER THIS FALL 59
CHAPTER 23: THE "PAT" BOX 60
CHAPTER 24: MOM'S HANDWRITING EMERGES 61
CHAPTER 25: THE ASIAN INVASION.......................................63
CHAPTER 26: WEATHERING THE RELATIVE SQUALOR...........65
CHAPTER 27: AS IF HE WERE YOGA AND I LUKE SKYWALKER
TRAINING ON THE DAGOBAH SYSTEM 66
CHAPTER 28: I WILL HAVE TO REQUIRE A FIRST-PLACE
VICTORY 68
CHAPTER 29: MY MOVIE'S MONTAGE 72
CHAPTER 30: LIKE A SHADOW ON ME ALL OF THE TIME 75
CHAPTER 31: LETTER #2 - NOVEMBER 15, 2006....................77
CHAPTER 32: LETTER #3 – NOVEMBER 18, 2006 78
CHAPTER33: LETTER #4 – NOVEMBER 29, 2006...................79
CHAPTER 34: LETTER #5 – DECEMBER 3, 2006.....................80
CHAPTER 35: LETTER #6 – DECEMBER 13, 2006....................81
CHAPTER 36: LETTER #7 – DECEMBER 14, 2006...................82

Chapter 37: The Square in My Hand 83
Chapter 38: Letter #8 – December 24, 2006 84
Chapter 39: An Episode Seems Inevitable 85
Chapter 40: Mad Nipper 87
Chapter 41: How is She? 89
Chapter 42: I Need a Huge Favor 91
Chapter 43: Best Intentions 93
Chapter 44: Booyah! 95
Chapter 45: Break Free of a Nimbostratus 96

About BookCaps

We all need refreshers every now and then. Whether you are a student trying to cram for that big final, or someone just trying to understand a book more, BookCaps can help. We are a small, but growing company, and are adding titles every month.

Visit www.bookcaps.com to see more of our books, or contact us with any questions.

Historical Context

First published in 2008, The Silver Linings Playbook is a story about sorrow, denial, acceptance, and, most of all, hope. Exploring classic literature, the importance of community, and "silver linings", this novel was birthed from Matthew Quick's personal journey.

In addition, The Silver Linings Playbook is also a tribute to Matthew Quick's hometown. Matthew was born and raised in Philadelphia, the City of Brotherly Love, and is a lifelong Eagles fan. He currently lives in South Jersey, just fifteen minutes away from the Lincoln Financial Field.

As a teenager, Matthew loved to write stories. He dreamed of becoming an author and writing for a living. However, he became convinced by the pessimism of the world that he could not make a living simply being an author. He settled instead for becoming a high school English teacher. As he talked to his students about the importance of following their dreams, and the potential their lives held, he came to realize that he needed to follow his own advice, follow his own dreams he had abandoned so long ago. He decided to set out on a journey across the world – he quit his job, sold his house and traveled around with nothing more than the pack on his back. He went white water rafting and walked across Africa. Eventually, he ended up in his in-laws basement writing full time, and thus The Silver Linings Playbook was born.

The Playbook is filled with hints of Matthew's own personal journey and discovery. Pat Peoples, in a way, IS Matthew Quick. Pat, like Matthew, was a high school teacher. He gains knowledge and learns lessons though the extensive reading of literature. Pat does not believe in pessimism, but, rather, chooses to believe that there is always some form of hope, however nontraditional and unexpected. He follows his desires to improve himself, just as Matthew followed his desires on his soul searching journey. And just as Pat improves himself through non-stop dedication and work out routines, most of which take place in his parents' basement, so too did Matthew Quick improve himself through writing, also in his in-laws' basement. It is no accident that The Silver Linings Playbook was the novel that was finished during this period of Matthew's life, and presents itself almost as a direct representation of the author.

When Matthew Quick quit his job, people thought he had gone crazy. Who would quit their job, sell their house, and backpack in Africa? They didn't believe his stories were ever going to amount to anything. He defeated their pessimism, producing a story that not only sold well and became a sweeping motion picture, but also served to illuminate the silver linings people miss in their everyday lives.

Plot Overview

Pat Peoples, a former high school history teacher, has just gotten out of the mental institution. He is taken back in by his family and lives his life waiting for his inevitable reunion with his wife, Nikki. He believes that Nikki and he are going through "apart time", and that if he improves himself enough, he will be able to be with her again.

Pat works out non-stop in his home gym located in his basement and runs ten miles a day at sunset. He always goes at sunset so he can watch the sky, and catch the silver lining on the clouds. This is his way of reminding himself that one day he will get Nikki back and that he can't give up hope.

When Pat first comes home, his Mom takes care of him and through careful planning, attempts to help Pat become a part of the family again. Soon after Pat's return home, the first Eagles game of the season comes on television. Pat's brother, Jake, comes over and gives Pat a welcome home present – a Hank Baskett jersey. Baskett is a new player with a lot of potential, and serves as a model of hope for Pat. Pat's father is at the game as well, although he doesn't talk to Pat at first.

On one of his evening runs, Pat is reunited with an old friend from school, Ronnie, who invites Pat over to dinner one evening. Ronnie is married to Veronica, and they have a toddler named Emily. Veronica's sister, Tiffany, also comes to dinner. Tiffany was married years ago, and her husband died. Pat walks Tiffany home, and they cry about their absent spouses.

Tiffany begins following Pat on his evening jogs, not saying anything, just following. Pat's therapist, Dr. Patel, or Cliff, encourages Pat to ask Tiffany out. They become friends and enjoy each other's silent company.

During this time, Pat is becoming closer to his father and brother through the Eagles football. Pat's Dad talks to him and leaves him the morning paper with the sports pages as a sign of goodwill. Jake takes Pat to see the Eagle's home games, and Pat becomes friends with many of the other tailgaters. Cliff is also an Eagles fan and becomes Pat's friend outside of their therapy sessions.

Tiffany reveals that she has been in contact with Nikki, who wants to talk to him through letters. Since there are restraining orders against both people, Tiffany will act as a liaison if Pat helps her win a dance competition. Pat must give up football for one month, and practice with Tiffany in her dance studio. They perform brilliantly, and everyone is proud of him.

Through Nikki's letters, Pat learns that she is remarried and has no desire to see him again. Pat asks her to meet at the place they became engaged, and Tiffany shows up instead. Tiffany made up the letters in an attempt to give Pat closure.

Pat remembers how he and Nikki separated, how she cheated on him, and he almost killed her lover. He woke up in the hospital with no memory of any of it. He goes to confront Nikki and realizes she is happy with her new family.

Although he gives up hope with Nikki, he realizes that Tiffany accepts him for all his faults, and that the two need each other.

Themes

Seeing the "Silver Lining"

Pat Peoples is obsessed with seeing the silver lining. After he leaves the mental institution, it is that image which represents hope for him. He goes running at dusk every day just so he can see the clouds, and be reminded that everything will work out. This blindly optimistic hope is what allows Pat to become a better person throughout the novel; it is what keeps him going when nothing else does. He eventually realizes that he cannot accomplish everything and that there are some things that can't be fixed. However, there is always another silver lining to be found in life, even when it is least expected.

Being Kind Instead of Right

Pat's marriage to Nikki fell apart over the years because he didn't treat her well. He wasn't home a lot, never considered her feelings, and was emotionally abusive. Because of all this, she cheated on him, and their marriage ended. When Pat transforms himself, being "kind instead of right" becomes his own personal motto. He consciously thinks about his decision and repeats the phrase to himself over and over. As a result of this, he learns to consider others and opens himself up to new experiences.

Importance of Friendship and Acceptance

One of the first things Pat's mom says to him when he comes home is that everybody needs friends. Pat learns this throughout the novel, when he becomes friends with Danny, Tiffany, Cliff, as well as the Eagles fans. When Tiffany first starts following him on his jogs, he is annoyed by it. However, they slowly become friends, and, when she stops following him, he ends up missing her. The end of the novel, Tiffany and Pat realize that they need each other; they need someone who can accept them for who they are, problems and all.

Mental Instability

It is not clear if Pat was always mentally unstable, or if his instability was brought about by his accident, but, throughout the novel, this is the issue Pat struggles with the most. He has emotional outbursts and trouble controlling his emotions. Tiffany is the only other character who has mental problems, and that is why she can accept and love Pat, because she understands, to some extent, what he's going through. Pat believes many of the other characters in the novel are cold, and that they can't understand how a mentally unstable person feels.

Denial

Both Tiffany and Pat have problems with denial about their past. Pat is in denial about the fact that Nikki is never coming back and spends his days longing for their reunion. His denial was so powerful, that he forcefully forgot the crime he committed against her lover. His method of humming to distract himself when uncomfortable stimuli remind him of his past with Nikki keeps him in denial. When Tiffany's husband died, Tiffany was in denial, and had sex with random men, imagining that he was coming back. At the end of the novel, both characters have come to terms with their problems and rid themselves of their denial.

Domestic Disputes

The Silver Linings Playbook does not shy away from showing the troubles of domestic life. This is seen most notably in the relationship between Pat's Mom and Dad. Dad is emotionally cold and stubborn and doesn't seem to care about Mom, but she puts up with him anyway. Eventually, she puts her foot down and establishes rules around the house. Tiffany told her husband that she didn't want to have so much sex, and started a series of events which led to his car crash. Pat caught Nikki cheating, and almost killed her new lover before being bashed in the head.

Literature as a Reflection of People

Throughout the novel, Pat reads the novels that Nikki taught in her American Literature class. There is a strong connection between the life of the authors and the book. For example, Hemingway and Plath's work mightily depressed Pat, as there were no silver linings at the end. Both of these authors committed suicide; Hemingway shot himself, and Plath stuck her head in the oven. By writing a novel which inspires hope, Matthew Quick draws a link between himself and his novel in a layer of self-reflection.

Movies and Visual Pictures

Pat believes that everyone's life is a series of movies. People encounter troubles, go through impossible times, and emerge victorious at the end. Pat no longer watches movies, because he is focusing on his own, and his reunion with Nikki will be his ending. There are several points where Pat even uses movie lingo to write his story. The best example of this is Pat's Own Montage, in which he uses a series of snippet events to mimic a movie montage. In the end, Pat decides the scene of Nikki laughing happily with her new family is a good end for his movie and begins a new chapter with Tiffany.

Sports and Physical Activity

Pat spends most of his days working out as a way to relieve his strong emotions, good and bad. When he's elated he runs farther and faster during his evening jog, and when he's depressed or angry he lifts weights. When he dances with Tiffany, she tells him to channel his sadness into movement. There is also the strong theme of Eagles football throughout. The football games bring Pat together with his family and establish a sense of immediate belonging with fellow fans.

Transformation

At the heart of this novel lies a traditional journey - not only for Pat, but for the author, as well. The novel chronicles the many transformations that people undergo in their lives. Pat has several distinct transformations during his journey. He begins as an emotionally absent husband, then the mentally ill patient, a man overcoming his denial, and finally a kind individual. Pat's personal journey made him a better person, and, in the end, he was thankful for everything he went through to get to that point. People never stop changing, and Pat hopes to change for the better.

Characters

Pat Peoples

Pat is a former high school history teacher who, at the beginning of the novel, just came home from a mental institution. He firmly believes that he and his wife are going through an "apart time" that will inevitably come to an end. He believes that if he becomes a decent enough person that Nikki will come back to him. He works out endlessly, running ten miles a day, and practices controlling his anger and being kind instead of right. He comes to realize that Nikki is never coming back, and that he is a better person because of his struggle with mental illness.

Tiffany

Introduced to Pat through her sister, Veronica, Tiffany becomes Pat's friend when he comforts her. She begins jogging with Pat and gets him to enter a dance competition with her. Eventually, she falls in love with him, and pretends to be Nikki to give him a sense of closure. Not good at communicating with people, she is blunt and straightforward. Her husband died a few years ago, and she became extremely depressed. She understands what Pat is going through and loves him in spite of, or perhaps because of, his illness.

Nikki

Pat's ex-wife. She and Pat met in college when they were children, and got married soon after. Eventually, she and Pat's marriage fell apart, and she cheated on him. She took his assets in the divorce, and is now happily married to another man and has two children. Nikki teaches high school English, and her friends are all literary. In an effort to impress Nikki when apart time is over, Pat begins reading all literature books Nikki taught in her classes. Pat only has one picture of Nikki and keeps it next to his face when he sleeps at night.

Cliff (Dr. Patel)

Pat's therapist and a fellow Eagles fan. Pat meets with Cliff every Friday afternoon for their weekly session. Pat thinks of him as the best therapist in the world, because he does not force Pat to be pessimistic. Cliff is part of a tailgating group called Asian Invasion, and he becomes friends with Pat outside of their therapy sessions through the Eagles football games. He seems to genuinely care about Pat and supports him throughout his journey to a better self.

Mom

Pat's mother is, at first, an obedient housewife. She cares deeply for all members of her family, and she was the one who fought so that Pat could leave the mental hospital. She buys him a home gym and takes care of him. She is constantly trying to get the family to be close again. Eventually she learns to stand up to her husband, and have a say about what goes on around the house. Pat knows that his mother will love him no matter what kind of person he is, and her acceptance means a lot to him.

Dad

Silent and stubborn, his moods are mostly based on whether or not the Eagles are winning their football games. For the first few weeks Pat is at home, Dad doesn't even talk to him. He first speaks to him while watching an Eagles game, and, through football, he comes to tolerate his mentally ill son. When he and Pat's mother begin having serious problems in their marriage, it takes him a long time to cave in to her demands. As a result, however, he must be more present in the family, and talk to Pat every day.

Jake

Pat's brother, also an Eagles fan. When they are reunited, Jake gives Pat his Hank Baskett jersey and season tickets to the football games. Although Pat does not know it at first, Jake is happily married to a musician named Caitlin. He does his best to tell his brother the truth and protects him fiercely when Tiffany pretends to be Nikki. Jake is always there to support Pat when he needs it and is the one who does Pat a monumental favor, driving him to Maryland to see Nikki.

Ronnie

One of Pat's old friends from school. Ronnie is married to Veronica, and his daughter is named Emily. At first Pat doesn't trust Ronnie because he never visited Pat and Nikki in Maryland, but Ronnie wrote to Pat while he was in the mental institution, giving him regular updates on his family and daughter. Ronnie is a fellow Eagles fan, and he and Pat bond over football. He also warns Pat about Nikki and tells him that she isn't normal.

Veronica

Ronnie's wife, Tiffany's older sister, and mother of Emily. Veronica tries to get Pat and Tiffany together by throwing a dinner party. She seems supportive of her sister and realizes that having a friend will be advantageous for Tiffany. Although she is wary of Pat's involvement with her sister, and worries about Tiffany's depression getting worse if she is rejected, Veronica ends up thankful to Pat and tells him that he has undoubtedly helped her sister.

Emily

Ronnie and Veronica's daughter. The last time Pat saw her before he went into the mental institution, Emily was just a baby. Now that she is a toddler, Pat feels a strange attraction to her. Every time he sees her, he imagines having children with Nikki. Emily called Pat "pap" and enjoys sitting in his lap. Although she can't speak much, Emily is a positive force for Pat, and some of his happiest moments in the book are when he is carefree and playing with Emily.

Caitlin

Jake's wife. Caitlin comes from a family of musicians, and she and Jake are in love. They got married while Pat was in the mental institution, and since Pat couldn't go to the wedding, no one told him his brother was married. After a while, Jake tells Pat about his wife, and they all go out to lunch. Caitlin is pretty, talented, and wants to be Pat's friend, if he will let her.

Scott

An old friend of Pat's from school. Scott has season tickets to all the Eagles games just like Jake and Pat. He goes to all the tailgating events, and is happy to see Pat again after so long. Since Pat entered the mental hospital, Scott got married and had two children. Scott and Jake are both popular at the Eagles games.

Danny

Pat's black friend from the mental hospital. When Danny first arrived, he didn't speak, but eventually he spoke to Pat. Throughout the story, Pat mentions slang that Danny taught him. On Christmas Day, the day after Danny got out of the mental hospital, he finds Pat on his front lawn after Pat was mugged. He takes Pat to the hospital and visits him regularly during his recovery. Their favorite activity is playing board games, and Danny always wins.

Dr. Timbers

Although Dr. Timbers only shows up in the first chapter, he remains a powerful force for Pat throughout his journey. To Pat, Dr. Timbers is the essence of pessimism, which Pat rails against in his search for his silver lining. When he meets Dr. Patel, he is immediately grateful that his new therapist is nothing like Dr. Timbers.

Hank Baskett

A rookie player for the Eagles, with a lot of potential to be great. Jake gets Pat a Hank Baskett jersey, and from then on Pat and Baskett become linked. During the tailgating events, Pat is often referred to as Baskett, and when Baskett is successful, everyone congratulates Pat. Pat wants Baskett to improve himself, just as Pat wants to improve himself.

Chapter Summary

Chapter 1: An Infinite Amount of Days until My Inevitable Reunion with Nikki

Pat is doing push-ups in the courtyard when his mother comes to visit. She asks him if he would like to come home, but he can only leave the institution if he promises not to look for Nikki. Pat wants to get away from the pessimistic doctors, so he agrees to come home, but only until his "apart time" with Nikki ends.

Pat says goodbye to his roommate and his doctor, and then gets in the car with his Mom. They drive back to his hometown, Collingswood, New Jersey. His mom tells him that she worked exceptionally hard to get him out of the institution, so he has to follow the rules carefully, or he will be forced to go back.

Going into town, there are many new buildings and people. Pat begins getting nervous and has to control his breathing to calm down.

As soon as they get home, Pat goes down to the basement. His Mom has filled it with brand-new workout equipment. He is so excited, he begins working out immediately. He spends his days working out and writing in his daily memoir so that when apart time is over, Nikki will know how he's been spending his days.

All the pictures of Pat and Nikki have been taken down. When he asks his mother, she says a burglar stole them. Pat doesn't believe her.

He doesn't see his father, who works a lot and spends time in his study.

Pat decides he wants to start reading books so he can salvage his marriage and impress Nikki's friends, who make fun of him for being stupid. His Mom uses her library card to get him books, and he asks for The Great Gatsby. He doesn't like it because the ending doesn't have a silver lining.

Chapter 2: He Does Not Preach Pessimism

Pat is working out when his Mom comes downstairs and tells him that he has an appointment with Dr. Patel.

In the waiting room, Pat hears "Songbird" by Kenny G. and starts yelling and throwing things around. Dr. Patel and his mother come in. Dr. Patel tells the secretary to turn the music off. Pat hides his face with his hands so they won't see him crying. Dr. Patel asks Pat to come into his office.

The office has a calming atmosphere, and the two relax in recliners. Pat doesn't want the doctor to think he's depressed. They begin talking, and Dr. Patel wants Pat to call him by his first name, Cliff.

Cliff asks about the song, and Pat closes his eyes and counts to ten. Cliff asks again, and Pat clears his mind again. Pat asks why Cliff wants to know about Nikki. Cliff knows that being reunited with Nikki is the main goal of Pat's life. Pat says he can't wait until apart time is over. He and Nikki decided to separate, and she was going to come back when she got her life figured out. Pat thinks she left because he was overweight and a workaholic. He wants her to come back soon, but he isn't allowed to contact Nikki or her family and doesn't remember why. He just believes that Nikki will come back.

Cliff doesn't tell Pat that Nikki won't come back to him like all the other doctors did, so Pat decides he likes Cliff. Pat thinks that life is like a series of movies, with the main character overcoming struggles and improving his life. Right now Pat is focusing on his own movie, and waiting for his happy ending, his reunion with Nikki.

They engage in small talk for a while longer, and Cliff tells Pat that he wants to change his medication.

On the way home, Pat tells his Mom that he thinks Nikki is going to come back soon, and his Mom begins crying.

Back at home, his father is still in his study, so Pat goes back to work out.

Chapter 3: Orange Fire Enters my Skull

Pat goes running every evening. He makes sure to go when the sun is setting, so he can see the silver lining on the clouds. The silver lining reminds him that Nikki is coming back.

Since apart time began, Pat's lost 50 pounds. He thinks Nikki got mad that he gained weight over the 5 years they were married.

When there are no clouds in the sky, Pat stares straight into the sun.

Chapter 4: The Worst Ending Imaginable

Pat asks for a Hemingway book because Nikki teaches it in her classroom. He wants one that's a love story. His Mom brings him A Farewell to Arms.

Pat is devastated by the ending in which the wife dies giving birth. He cries uncontrollably and thinks if Hemingway was alive he would kill him.

Chapter 5: Got Nothin' but Love for Ya

When Pat enters Dr. Patel's waiting room, the secretary turns the music off. In the office, Patel asks about the medicine. Pat says it's fine, but doesn't admit he's spitting them out whenever he gets the chance. Patel asks about any unwanted side effects, specifically, hallucination. Pat says he hasn't had any.

At home, Pat smells Mom cooking. She is making crabby cakes, Nikki's favorite food. He hopes that apart time is over, but instead his Mom tells him his brother, Jake, is coming to watch the game.

To clear his head, Pat goes for a run. He passes an old friend named Ronnie, and ignores him. Ronnie never visited Pat and Nikki in Baltimore.

Jake is at the house, and he can't believe how ripped Pat is. Jake bought him an Eagles jersey, number 84, Hank Baskett. He also bought Pat season tickets to make up for all the time they've spent apart.

Chapter 6: The Concrete Doughnut

Father ignores Pat, and everyone starts eating. As they watch, Pat inexplicably remembers people's names. The Eagles are playing at the Lincoln Financial Field, and Pat thought they played at Veteran's Stadium. When he asks what happened, Jake tells him the stadium was demolished, and shows him a video of the demoliton. Pat thinks he is hallucinating and is in disbelief when his Mom reveals that it was demolished in 2006, four years ago.

Pat starts freaking out and shakes his Mom, asking her how long he was in the bad place. Jake tells him four years, and Pat lets go of his mother. He hears Mom scream, and his head hits the ground.

Chapter 7: I Fear Him More Than Any Other Being

Sleeping in the attic, Pat hallucinates that Kenny G. is singing "Songbird" to him. Pat screams for Kenny to stop. His mother and father are restraining him, and his Mom gets knocked to the floor. Dad begins punching him in the face and the hallucination vanishes. Pat starts crying, and his Mom holds him, stroking his hair until he falls asleep.

Pat wakes up with Mom still stroking his hair. She cooks him breakfast, and he takes his pills before starting his morning workout.

Chapter 8: The Dress-Up Dinner

In the basement, Ronnie comes to visit Pat. He admires the gym and wants to work out with him sometime. Pat says yes, but thinks Ron won't keep his promise.

Ronnie apologizes for never visiting him in Baltimore, and invites Pat over to dinner. His wife, Veronica, wants Pat to dress nice for the occasion.

After Ron leaves, Pat thinks what Nikki would say about the dinner, and how much she hates Veronica.

Chapter 9: If I Backslide

Pat worries about what to wear to dinner. He forgets its Friday, his appointment day with Dr. Patel.

In the office, Pat tells Patel about his problem. Dr. Patel suggests that he wear his new jersey. He tries to ask Pat about Kenny G. again, but Pat keeps avoiding the question. Dr. Patel tells Pat that he was rough with his Mom this week, and, if the outbursts continue, he'll have to go back to the institution.

Pat cries uncontrollably, saying he wants to be a decent person, and he'll try harder. He'll do anything to avoid going back to the bad place.

Chapter 10: I Don't Know How This Works

After lifting and running weights, Pat showers and gets ready for the dinner. His mom suggests he wear a polo shirt instead of the jersey, but Pat doesn't want to.

Ronnie answers the door in a jacket and tie, but compliments Pat on the jersey. Inside, Veronica is feeding Emily, no longer a newborn. Pat thinks about having kids with Nikki.

Veronica's sister, Tiffany, is also coming to dinner. Her husband Tommy died a while back. She arrives all dressed up, and Pat tries to make awkward small talk with her, but she walks out of the room.

During dinner, Veronica and Ron do all the talking. They try to make plans for the four of them to go out. Right after dinner, Tiffany says she is tired and wants Pat to walk her home. She lives with her parents down the street. When they get to her house, she says she doesn't know how this dating thing works, but they can have sex if Pat wants.

Pat says he is married, showing her the ring. She shows him her ring, and they both begin crying.

Back at home, Mom said Ronnie called. Pat doesn't call him back, and stares at the ceiling until the sun comes up.

Chapter 11: Filled with Molten Lava

Pat has one picture of Nikki, a headshot taken at a photo shoot. It was a Christmas present, and when he got it he didn't like it. He kisses the glass and thinks about their wedding. He decides he wants to watch the wedding video and asks his parents where it is. They say they don't have it, but he looks for it anyway. When he can't find it, he gets angry and works out to burn off some steam.

Pat goes to sleep with the picture of Nikki lying next to his head.

Chapter 12: Failing like Dimmesdale Did

Pat just finished reading The Scarlet Letter. He doesn't approve of most of the characters, but loves Hester because she believes in silver linings. He thinks it's crucial to treat women well, and wishes he would have treated Nikki better.

Chapter 13: Do You Like Foreign Films?

Cliff asks how the dinner party went, and especially about Tiffany. Pat tells Cliff she was slutty, because she asked to have sex. Cliff wants to know why Pat didn't have sex with her, and Pat says it is because he loves his wife, Nikki.

Tiffany has been following Pat on his jogging route every day. She somehow knows his schedule, and Pat can't get rid of her. Cliff asks Pat how long it's been since he's seen Nikki, and why not give Tiffany a chance. Pat yells at Cliff and then calms down.

Cliff asks Pat if he likes foreign films. Cliff's wife used to love them, and bugged him all the time about going. After taking her to a few, she stopped asking. He suggests doing the same thing with Tiffany and asking her out on a date.

Chapter 14: I Can Share Raisin Bran

In the car on the way home, Pat's Mom offers to give him some money if he wants to take Tiffany out. During their jog, Pat asks Tiffany to dinner, and she agrees to go.

Mom bought Pat new clothes, and makes sure he looks good. She gives him money and tells him to have an enjoyable time. Tiffany is waiting outside her house, and they walk to a diner.

Pat worries about not having enough money, and orders Raisin Bran because it's the cheapest thing on the menu. He notices that Tiffany didn't order anything, and offers to share his cereal. She refuses, and Pat leaves the waitress a large tip.

On the walk home, Tiffany takes back what she said to Pat about being able to have sex with her, and then goes inside her house. Back at his own house, Pat ignores his mother and goes up to the attic where the picture of Nikki is. Pat talks to Nikki for a while before falling asleep crying.

Chapter 15: Sing and Spell and Chant

It is game day, so Pat gets up early to run. Tiffany is waiting for him, even though he didn't tell her he was running early. She acts like they never went out to dinner and follows him like normal.

After the ten mile run, Pat takes a shower and puts on his Hank Bassett jersey. Downstairs, his brother, dad, and Ronnie are all in the living room. They begin singing the Eagles fight song, and Pat feels at home for the first time. He's glad that his father can be in the same room as him.

During halftime, the boys go outside to play catch. Dad keeps nodding approvingly, and Pat is happy the Eagles are ahead. They end up winning, and in the final group chant his father touches him with his arm.

Ronnie wants Pat to walk him home, and they stop at the park for some more catch. Ron asks Pat about Tiffany and warns him that she is odd. He says she's seeing a therapist and tells Pat why she was fired from her job. Pat thinks the whole time that Ron doesn't understand what she was going through and that it's wrong to judge her. He sympathizes with her.

After Ronnie leaves, Pat goes to Tiffany's parents and knocks on the door. Tiffany's mom opens the door, and Pat asks if he can see her daughter. Tiffany's mom questions Pat's intentions, and Pat insists that they're just friends and shows her the wedding ring on his finger to prove it.

Tiffany is out back, and Pat asks why she keeps following him. She answers that she's scouting him, but won't say what for.

Chapter 16: The Best Therapist in the Entire World

The day after the game, Pat's father visits him in the basement. He brings Pat the newspaper with the sports section, and wants Pat to follow up on the new players. He is going to leave the newspaper on the top step every morning. It is a tremendous deal, because, as a kid, Dad always took the paper to work with him, and never let Jake or Pat read it.

Mom cooks Pat breakfast, and seems happy. Every night when Dad comes home, Pat hopes he will talk about the Eagles, but he doesn't.

Pat tells Cliff about the newspaper, but Cliff wants to talk about Tiffany. Pat is going to the beach with Ronnie, Veronica, Emily and Tiffany, and Cliff wants to know if Pat is looking forward to seeing Tiffany in a bikini.

After their session, Cliff does the Eagles chant with Pat, and Pat thinks he's the best therapist in the world.

Chapter 17: Tiffany's Head Floating over the Waves

Ronnie picks up Pat in the family Minivan. Veronica, Tiffany and Emily are already in. Pat's Mom tries to make small talk, and Tiffany ignores her. Pat feels like a five year old.

At the beach, no one else is there. Emily gets sand in her eye and begins crying. Tiffany gets upset, and Veronica reminds her about what her therapist said. Tiffany doesn't want Veronica to bring up her therapist in front of Pat, and storms off. Veronica follows, leaving Emily with Pat and Ron.

Ron falls asleep under the umbrella, and Pat takes Emily swimming. They are floating with the waves, going deeper into the ocean. Emily is laughing, and Pat is happy. Suddenly Veronica is yelling at Pat, who swims back to shore. Emily starts crying when she sees her mother yelling, and Veronica accuses Ron of leaving Emily alone with "him".

Pat takes off running. He is crying. He was so happy swimming with Emily, and he didn't do anything wrong. It wasn't right for Veronica to get so mad. Tiffany passes him, and Pat begins racing her. Pat gets ahead, and they jog together for a while. Tiffany goes out into the ocean, and Pat follows. They float together, not talking, and Pat gets the urge to kiss her.

Back by the van, they tell Veronica and Ron that they want to go home.

Chapter 18: A Hive Full of Green Bees

Pat wakes up to his Dad by his bedside, shouting the Eagles chant. The big game is today, and Jake and Pat are using their season tickets. Pat gets up early to work out and run before Dad drives him to the stadium. They talk in the car about football, and the importance of putting family first.

At the stadium, there are people in Eagle jerseys everywhere. Pat looks at where the Veteran Stadium used to be, but it isn't there anymore. He finds his brother at a tailgating tent, and his old friend Scott is there. Since Scott has seen Pat last, he got married and had two little girls. Pat does the mental math in his head, and he hasn't seen Scott in four years. He decides to ignore this, he doesn't want to think about it too much.

A man in a Giants jersey walks in, with a little boy. Jake begins calling the man an Asshole and starts up a chant. The boy gets scared and starts crying. The Giants fan singles out Pat, and shoves him, even though Pat wasn't chanting. Jake tries to get him to stop, but the Giants fan throws him to the ground. Pat sees Jake is bleeding and punches the guy out. Someone says to call an ambulance, and Pat runs away as fast as he can. He keeps throwing up and crying.

Eventually Jake catches up to him; he is on the phone, and the Giants fan wakes up and is pissed. Pat shouldn't come back to the tent. Pat feels unbelievably guilty about what happened, but Jake told him he was defending his family, and he's a hero for that.

They go to the game, and the Eagles lose. Back at the house, Pat's Dad has broken the television set. Pat goes to work out, but keeps thinking about the kid crying, and punching his dad out. He falls asleep and dreams about the crying boy turning into Nikki, who says that she hates him. Pat doesn't like these uncontrollable actions, and losing his temper.

In the morning, there is a copy of the morning paper on the top step of the basement.

Chapter 19: Sister Sailor Mouth

A couple of days after the game, Pat is eating dinner with Tiffany at the diner. They are sharing Raisin Bran. Pat thinks Tiffany looks sad. He tells her about what happened with the Giant's fan, and Tiffany doesn't understand why Pat feels guilty. He says it's because Nikki is a pacifist, and Tiffany says to fuck Nikki. She begins yelling and gets kicked out of the diner for cursing.

Pat pays the bill and goes outside after her, only to see her jogging away. He follows her to her house, but she doesn't even say goodbye.

Chapter 20: The Implied Ending

Pat tries to read The Bell Jar by Sylvia Plath. It interests him because the main character has mental health problems, and he wants to know how she fixes them. The ending implies that she might get better, but he finds out the book is Plath's memoir, and she killed herself.

He gets mad, rips the book in half, and goes to work out.

The next day, Tiffany follows Pat on his evening jog as usual, and they don't say anything about the night before.

Chapter 21: An Acceptable Form of Coping

Pat spills everything to Cliff about the Giants fan, the crying boy, Tiffany, and Sylvia Plath. Cliff stands up out of his chair, and gives Pat a pep talk about the Giants fan, saying he deserved it. When he sits back down, he says he is the therapist again, and talks to Cliff about finding an alternative to using violence to solve issues. He recommends Pat try the humming technique he uses whenever Kenny G. is mentioned.

Cliff thinks Tiffany is jealous of Pat's love for Nikki, and that The Bell Jar is an extremely depressing book. Before Pat leaves, Cliff does the Eagles chant with him again.

Chapter 22: Balanced Very Carefully, As If the Whole Thing Might Topple When the Heater Vents Begin to Blow Later this Fall

In the basement, Pat hears a new television. Dad replaced the one he broke, and Mom is upset because they don't have the money. Pat realizes this is his fault and feels guilty. He hears Mom leave the house, and Dad is watching a game.

Pat goes upstairs, and compliments Dad on the new TV. Dad ignores him. The television is enormous, bigger than the end table and perched precariously. Pat goes jogging, and when he comes back Mom still isn't home.

Chapter 23: The "Pat" Box

At eleven, Pat begins to worry because Mom isn't back yet. He takes his medications because he wants to please her.

When she pulls in the drive, she is drunk. Pat helps her inside and carries her to his bed. He gets her water and makes her take a Tylenol.

Pat sleeps up in the attic and hallucinates that Kenny G. is standing on top of him. He tries the humming technique, but Kenny G. is still there. He tries it several more times, and Kenny G. disappears. Pat is ecstatic and searches the attic to make sure he's quite gone. In the corner, he finds a box labeled "Pat". He opens it, and immediately wishes he hadn't. He puts it back where it was and tries to pretend he didn't see it, but now he's upset at Mom.

Chapter 24: Mom's Handwriting Emerges

Pat wakes up to the smell of something burning. Downstairs, Dad is trying to cook steak. The fire alarm goes off, and Pat searches for his morning pills. Dad begins to watch football, and Pat goes to work out.

Midmorning Mom comes down to the basement. Pat doesn't want to talk to her, because he is still mad about what he found in the box. Mom says there are going to be some changes around the house, and that she is going out today.

It is game day, so Pat decides to go running early. He wants to see Tiffany, but she isn't there. Back at the house, Jake isn't there either, so it is just Pat and Dad watching the game. Dad doesn't talk to Pat, and, at halftime, they order pizza. The Eagles win, and Dad is in a little better mood. They do the Eagles chant, and Dad leaves without saying anything else.

Pat is practicing being kind, so he cleans up the house. He finds a note with Mom's handwriting on it. It is for his Dad, telling him to either return the television or spend more time with Pat and Mom. If he doesn't do one of these things, Mom will go on strike.

Pat calls Jake and a woman answers the phone. She puts Jake on the line, and Jake tells Pat Mom didn't want him to come to the game. She told Ronnie not to come either, to give Pat and Dad some alone time. Pat reads the note to Jake, and Jake is proud of Mom for standing up to Dad.

Pat is still cleaning when Mom comes home. She tells him he doesn't need to do that, because they're not cleaning until Dad gets his act together. Pat asks if Jake has a girlfriend, because a girl answered the phone. Mom says he might, but doesn't say anything else. Pat wonders if she is hiding even more from him.

Chapter 25: The Asian Invasion

It's game day again, and Pat goes to Jake's apartment. Jake lives in a high-rise and has a nice television and grand piano. Pat didn't know Jake played, and Jake tells Pat that it's Caitlin's piano. He is happily married, but didn't want to tell Pat because he knows how much Pat misses Nikki. Jake wants Pat to meet her, so they go to lunch.

Caitlin is a musician, and, over sandwiches, Pat asks about the ceremony and how long they've been married. Caitlin's answer is vague. She wants to become his friend.

On the way to the game, Pat asks what Jake does for a living. He says he trades stock. Pat wants to tell Jake about all his problems, but he doesn't.

At the tailgating tent, there is a bus labeled Asian Invasion who wants them to move. Pat recognizes Cliff on the bus, and tells everyone to move the tents. When everyone is settled, Cliff brings over food and they end up drinking beer together as friends. They play a Swedish Viking game, and Cliff is Pat's partner. After the game, Pat gets a ride home in the Asian Invasion bus.

He lifts weights to burn off the tailgating food, and so he won't think about missing his brother's wedding.

Chapter 26: Weathering the Relative Squalor

Pat tells Mom about meeting Caitlin. Mom is glad and hangs their wedding pictures back up. Pat remembers his own wedding and wants his pictures up. He found them in the attic, in the "Pat" box. He asks Mom why she lied to him, and she doesn't answer.

Chapter 27: As If He Were Yoga and I Luke Skywalker Training on the Dagobah System

At Cliff's office, Pat talks about the upcoming game. The Eagles are playing the Cowboys, and a player called Terrence had a suicide attempt. He used to play for the Eagles, and switched teams. Pat overheard his dad call Terrence a "psychopathic pill popper", and it hurt Pat's feelings because he feels sympathy for Terrence.

At the game, everyone is selling homemade anti-Terrence shirts and propaganda, and chanting, making fun of his pill-popping and suicide attempt. Pat is distracted, and Cliff takes him inside the bus, sitting down in the pleather seat. He asks Pat what's wrong, and Pat tells Cliff that all the anti-Terrence stuff is bothering him. He would feel bad if thousands of people were making fun of his mental problems. Cliff assures him that it's all in good fun, and Terrence is making lots of money off the publicity.

During the game, Hank Baskett scores his first touchdown in an NFL game. Pat is lifted on everyone's shoulders, and back at the tailgating area everyone celebrates the Eagles victory. Pat is so happy and is sad when the Asian Invasion bus drops him off at home. Inside, he expected to see his Dad waiting for him, but the house is clean and Mom and Dad aren't there. Pat knocks on their bedroom door, and realizes he interrupted them.

Pat decides to get out of the house and knocks on Tiffany's door. They go walking, and Pat tells her about everything that happened that day. Tiffany listens, and, at the end of their walk, she hands him an envelope. She tells him that he has to wait 48 hours to open it, and he has to be in a happy mood when he does. She says she expects an answer soon, and that she can be a close friend, or an enemy. Pat remembers the story Ronnie told him about how Tiffany got fired, and is afraid.

Chapter 28: I Will Have to Require a First-Place Victory

Dad is submitting to Mom's terms, and Pat, Mom and Dad are sharing a family dinner. Dad is asking Pat questions about the football season and then asks about Tiffany. He is under the impression that Tiffany is Pat's girlfriend, and he should meet her. Jake told Dad Pat was over Nikki, but Pat gets uncomfortable when Dad asks these questions and goes to lift weights. Pat is disappointed because he wanted to open the letter tonight, but now he's not in a good mood.

Instead of opening the letter, Pat goes running. He runs faster and faster, motivating himself with his desire to see Nikki. When he gets back to the house, his parents are asleep, and since he is in a jolly mood he decides to open the letter.

At the beginning of the letter, Tiffany has a few points. 1) Pat must read the letter through to the end, 2) After reading the letter, Pat has to burn it, and 3) Pat has to give her an answer within 24 hours of opening it. Pat continues reading.

When Tiffany lost Tommy (her husband) she became mentally unstable. Originally, she thought Pat was going to be a replacement for Tommy, but after seeing Pat's profound love for Nikki and his all-encompassing desire to see her, she changed her mind. She thinks God sent her to Pat to help the apart time be over.

Tiffany found Nikki's phone number and has been talking to her for the past couple of weeks. Turns out, Nikki still misses Pat. Not as much as he misses her, but she would like to get in contact with him. Four years ago, Pat committed a crime which he no longer remembers. As a result, Nikki filed for divorce, received all Pat's assets, and Pat had to go for a checkup at the mental institution. Just when Pat's doctor was about to release him for being mentally stable, Pat forgot the crime he had committed, and was forced to stay in the hospital much longer than originally planned. After the crime, Nikki's family filed a restraining order against Pat, and when Pat stayed in the mental hospital, his family filed a restraining order against Nikki. As a result, neither of them are legally allowed to contact the other.

Tiffany is willing to act as a liaison for them to write letters to the other, two per week. Her condition is that Pat must help her win a dance competition. Pat is the strongest man she's ever seen, and she doesn't think it's an accident that they met. She needs a strong man to do the lifts she has in mind during the routine. If they win first place, Tiffany will deliver letters to and from Nikki. If they don't win, Pat will have lost his only chance. In order to win, Pat must give up the Eagles for the month before the competition, and practice with Tiffany constantly.

After reading the letter, Pat thinks all night. He wonders whether it is true or not; maybe Tiffany is just making up a story to get him to do the dance competition with her. In the end, he decides that it isn't important – if it's a chance to see Nikki, then it's worth everything.

When the sun comes up, Pat jogs over to Tiffany's house and knocks on her room. She answers the door in a nightgown, and asks Pat if he's in. Pat says yes.

They go to Tiffany's dance studio, and Tiffany gives Pat a pair of headphones. She tells him to listen to the song they will be dancing to, and to hold his picture of Nikki. The stronger the connection to the song, the better the dance will be.

The song is painfully sad, and, at the end of it, Pat realizes he is crying. He's embarrassed, but Tiffany says he needs to put his sadness into movement in order to win.

Chapter 29: My Movie's Montage

Pat can't write in detail about the dance practices, because Tiffany closely guards her methods. Since she is aiming to be a dance teacher, she doesn't want people to steal her strategies.

Pat is reminded of those sports movies where pictures flit across the screen. In the span of just a few minutes, the audience gets a taste of everything that happens while all the while realizing that a lot of work and time is passing.

At Cliff's office, Pat asks him what that is called. Cliff answers a montage. The rest of the chapter is short "clips" of Pat's month – his own montage.

Tiffany and Pat run a little faster every day. He always wins, partly because he's a guy, but also because he's a terrific runner.

Dad wants to know why Pat is humming every time Dad mentions football. He thinks Pat is going crazy again.

Jake calls on the telephone; upset that Pat isn't going to the Eagles game.

Tiffany tells Pat that it's normal to touch another person while you're dancing with them. Pat isn't touching her in a sexual way, it's just modern dance.

Cliff also is baffled by Pat's humming. He wants Pat to go to the home game with everybody, and to tell him what is going on.

Mom wants Pat to take a break and says that Pat is undoing all the hard work she put into getting Dad and Jake to like Pat again.

Pat is working out, lifting weights and sweating. He and Tiffany are running farther every day.

Ronnie wants to know what Tiffany is holding over Pat. He warns Pat that she is capable of anything and that Pat shouldn't trust her.

Tiffany's dancing is the most beautiful thing Pat has ever seen. It's so sad and lovely.

Veronica visits Pat in the basement and tells him how much this means to Tiffany. She hasn't let anyone watch her dance since Tommy's dance, and she has invited the whole family to the rehearsal.

Pat kisses Nikki's picture before he goes to bed.

The Eagles have lost three games in a row. Dad is upset and blames Pat for the losses.

Tiffany buys Pat a pair of yellow tights. She also shaves his chest, because he won't be wearing a shirt. The razor tickles.

Their dance is almost perfect; the only thing missing is a large audience. Tiffany says that the audience can sway the judges.

Pat is working out, lifting more than ever before. He beats Tiffany easily in running.

Pat asks Cliff to come to the dance competition, and Cliff wants to know why. Pat can't give him an answer because of Tiffany's conditions, so he says he will tell Cliff after the competition. Cliff says he may or may not come.

Calling Jake, Pat leaves a message on the answering machine. He calls again, and Caitlin picks up the phone. He doesn't know what to do so he hangs up.

Mom says she'll come to the competition, but not to get her hopes up about Dad.

Chapter 30: Like a Shadow on Me All of the Time

Veronica drops Pat and Tiffany off at the hotel. Inside there is a dance hall, with a poster reading Dance Away Depression. As they are waiting to register, Pat is nervous. The other contestants arrive, and they are all young. Tiffany gives the workers the music to play, and they go backstage to change. Pat stays in the supply closet until all the teenage girls are changed. While he's back there, he worries someone might play a Kenny G. song, but Tiffany assures him no one is.

On stage, everyone is introduced. Pat looks out at the audience but doesn't see Cliff, Dad or Jake. He hopes Mom will show up. Pat and Tiffany are going last.

Finally, it is their turn to go on stage. Their song starts playing; it is "Turn Around, Bright Eyes." Pat knows the routine by heart, and Tiffany gives the dance her all. Pat is representative of the sun, and sets when Tiffany "dies". When the song fades, the applause is thunderous. Pat looks up and sees everyone in the back rows. Jake and Scott brought the whole Asian Invasion to cheer him on.

Backstage, Tiffany kisses Pat and hugs him for a long time. She tells him there is no trophy – she just said that to make him motivated. Pat asks if he can talk about football again, and Tiffany says he can do whatever he wants.

The Asian Invasion has planned an all-night tailgating party for the next day's game. They stay up late drinking and playing sports.

In the morning, Pat finds out everyone fell asleep on the bus. He is happy to be surrounded by all of his friends.

Chapter 31: Letter #2 - November 15, 2006

Pat receives his first letter from Nikki. She says they never got to talk; everything ended so abruptly. They never had a sense of closure. Pat sent Tiffany his entire diary, so Tiffany didn't get to tell Nikki everything. Nikki complains about working at the high school, and wants Pat to send a shorter letter next time.

Nikki is remarried. She was going to divorce Pat anyway, even before everything happened. He was a lousy husband, never home, not attentive. She cheated on him, which he forgot in the bad place.

She is impressed he read all those books, and is sorry they were depressing. She recommends Huck Finn, because it has a happy ending. She says literature is so sad because real life is sad. She admires the hard work he's put into getting help.

Chapter 32: Letter #3 – November 18, 2006

Pat checked out Huck Finn and read it all in one night. He enjoyed the ending, and thinks Nikki is sending him a message of hope.

When he read her letter, he cried. He knows he was a terrible husband, and he doesn't blame her for cheating or divorcing him. He tells Nikki he is a better person now and reminds her of the happy times they shared. All he wants is one more chance, and he still loves her.

Chapter33: Letter #4 – November 29, 2006

Nikki can tell he's downright transformed by his letters. However, there was no hidden message in Huck Finn. She recommends he read Catcher in the Rye because it is about a young boy who has trouble grasping reality.

She believes Pat is going through a second childhood, and she is no longer a child. She loves her current husband, and never wanted to give Pat a second chance; she only wanted to say goodbye.

Chapter 34: Letter #5 – December 3, 2006

In all the movies, the main character goes through a point where nothing looks like it's going to work out. Pat believes this is that time in his story.

Nikki's letter made him sad. He read some of it to Cliff, who said that Nikki and he were incompatible. Tiffany is a much better match. But Tiffany is not Pat's true love.

Pat read Catcher in the Rye, and wants to see Nikki face-to-face.

Chapter 35: Letter #6 – December 13, 2006

Nikki says Pat put Tiffany in an awkward situation in the last letter, because Tiffany obviously cares about him. Cliff was right to say that Nikki and Pat were incompatible. Nikki says that they are not getting anywhere and that this will be the last letter. Goodbye.

Chapter 36: Letter #7 – December 14, 2006

Pat worked too hard to give up now. He wants Nikki to meet him at the place where he proposed, at dusk, on Christmas day. This is the last thing he will ever ask of Nikki.

Chapter 37: The Square in My Hand

On Christmas Eve, Mom and Pat go to mass. Pat prays for a miracle for Nikki to show up tomorrow. He thanks God for sending him to the bad place, so he could become a better person. He also prays for the Eagles to win this season so his Dad might love him again.

When they get home Dad is asleep, so Mom and Pat hang out by the Christmas tree, and Mom tells stories about all the ornaments. Pat realizes his Mom will love him no matter what, and it makes him feel comforted.

Suddenly the doorbell rings. Pat hopes that it will be Nikki, but it is Ronnie and family come to carol at their door. Mom invites everyone in, and Pat gives presents to Ronnie, Veronica, Emily and Tiffany. They get Pat a picture of Hank Baskett with a personalized signature on it.

As they are leaving, Tiffany kisses Pat on the cheek, and grabs his hand. When she leaves, Pat has a small square piece of paper. When he goes to bed, he unfolds it.

Chapter 38: Letter #8 – December 24, 2006

Nikki is not coming. She never will. The restraining order is still in effect.

Chapter 39: An Episode Seems Inevitable

Christmas Day Pat wakes up optimistic. He exercises, and Mom cooks breakfast. They all sit around the Christmas tree and open presents. After, Pat tells his parents that he is going on a run. In truth, he is going to meet Nikki.

He goes out to the garage and changes into one of his father's old suits, sneaking out of the house and taking a train to Philadelphia. He makes his way through the city, the college campus, until he finally ends up under a tree overlooking a traditional teahouse. It was one of Nikki's favorite places to go. He waits there until dusk. It gets dark, and Nikki still hasn't shown up. Pat prays to God as hard as he can and hears a voice.

The voice isn't Nikki's, its Tiffany's. She's sorry things happened like this, and never thought Pat would go this far. She pretended to be Nikki to try and give Pat some closure, but she says everything in the letter, about Nikki being remarried and the restraining order, is true.

Pat wants to know why, and Tiffany says it's because she loves him. Pat runs away as fast as he can; Tiffany can't keep up. He cries and curses God as he runs, until something knocks him over and he is being kicked.

Chapter 40: Mad Nipper

When Pat wakes up, all of his stuff is gone, and it's hard to move his leg. He looks around; he's in a pretty crummy neighborhood. He thinks he was mugged because he cursed out God, and his eyes fall on a nativity scene across the lawn. He manages to get over to it and is holding baby Jesus when someone comes out on the front porch.

It is a true miracle – his friend from the institution, Danny. When Danny first came to the institution he wouldn't talk to anybody, but he talked to Pat. He told him his street name was Map Nipper. He was raised a rapper gangster in Baltimore and was thrown into the river by a bunch of other gangsters. Eventually, he ended up in the institution. He got his speech back, but not his ability to rap.

Danny invites him in for Christmas dinner. When Danny's Aunt comes in, she immediately takes him to the hospital, where he gets cleaned up and his leg put in a cast. Pat's family shows up there. Tiffany had called them to tell them what happened, and everyone is mad at her.

Mom, Dad and Jake take Pat out of the hospital. On the drive home, Pat feels guilty for ruining everyone's Christmas. He thinks the muggers should have gone ahead and killed him, because all he does is cause trouble for his family. He cries and apologizes, but no one says anything.

Chapter 41: How is She?

Pat's birthday is December 29th. Since his leg has been hurt, he hasn't done anything but stay in bed all day. Mom has to help him shower, and he doesn't even want to work out.

At Cliff's office, Pat tells him everything that happened. The only good thing that happened out of the whole ordeal was Danny comes to visit him now. They spend their time playing board games. Cliff asks Pat if he knows how he lost his memory. Everyone else does, and Cliff thinks Pat does too, he just doesn't want to admit it. He says although Tiffany's methods weren't right, it is true that Pat needs closure because real life is not a movie. Pat gets angry and yells at Cliff.

On the drive home, Pat asks Mom if Nikki is coming to his birthday party today. Mom tells him that Nikki is never coming. However, Jake, Caitlin, Ronnie, Veronica, and Emily all come. Emily draws a picture on his cast, and Pat receives lots of presents. He is thirty-five.

After he's done opening presents, he asks how Tiffany is. Everyone is silent, and then they start arguing amongst themselves. Pat asks again.

Chapter 42: I Need a Huge Favor

It is New Year's Eve Day. There is a game today, and Pat goes with Scott and Jake. They say they have to leave early because their wives have plans. Pat guilts Jake into staying. Hank Baskett ends up setting a record for the Eagles, and Pat is proud.

After the game, Jake leaves, and the two hug. Pat gets a ride home on the Asian Invasion bus and eats dinner with Mom and Dad. After dinner Mom and Pat watch the New Year's celebration at Times Square, and Mom falls asleep on the couch. Pat gets up to get her a blanket and finds his wedding video.

It starts at their reception, and "Songbird" by Kenny G. starts playing. Suddenly, Pat remembers a rainy day driving home in his car. When he enters the house, he hears "Songbird". In the bathroom the shower is running, and there are two sets of clothes. He strangles Nikki's lover, and Nikki bashes his head with the CD player. Pat falls, hitting his head on the faucet. He wakes up in the hospital, calling for Nikki, but she doesn't come.

The tape ends, and Pat is staring at his reflection in the television set.

He gets up and calls Jake. He leaves him a message, saying he needs a whopping favor.

Chapter 43: Best Intentions

Letter from Tiffany, because she is better at writing than talking to people. She apologizes for what she did, and says that she loves Pat. She wants to tell him the story of her husband Tommy, and how he died.

Tommy was a cop, a good man. He counseled teens and started a anti-drinking-and-driving club at the local high school. Their relationship was perfect, except for one thing – they had sex too much. At first Tiffany loved it, but after ten years having sex several times a day got to be too much. She told him she wanted to enjoy sex again, and he was hurt. He walked out of the house without saying goodbye.

An hour later Tiffany got a call from the hospital. Tommy had died, killed by a drunk driver. In the backseat of his car was a bag full of lingerie, all Tiffany's size.

Tiffany felt unbelievably guilty that her husband died believing she didn't want to have sex with him. She began having sex with any man she could, and imagining Tommy coming home.

When she met Pat at the dinner party, she thought he would be an easy lay; but when Pat simply held her when she cried, it turned into something else. Tiffany liked being friends with Pat, and soon became jealous whenever Pat talked about Nikki. Tiffany got Pat's Mom drunk to learn the true story about what happened, and they ended up becoming friends.

Tiffany misses Pat and wants to still be friends.

Chapter 44: Booyah!

Pat shows the letter to Danny while they are playing board games. Danny doesn't tell Pat what he thinks. He's a fantastic board game player, and hardly ever loses.

Chapter 45: Break Free of a Nimbostratus

It is a week after Pat's cast has been removed. He's standing on the bridge at the park, staring into the ice. Part of him wishes he hadn't regained his memories of Nikki. He sees Tiffany walking towards him in the distance, she accepted his invitation.

When she arrives, Pat asks her why she didn't come to his birthday. She reminds him that Jake threatened to kill her if she tried to see Pat again. Tiffany apologizes for everything, and is sorry that she isn't Nikki.

Pat tells Tiffany that he remembered everything, and decided to confront Nikki. Jake drove him out to the old house in Maryland, and Pat saw Nikki outside playing in the snow with her new family. She had a loving husband, and two children and was smiling. Pat decided that was a superb picture for his story to end on, and he left without talking to her.

When he finishes telling Tiffany, he realizes he is crying. Tiffany got him a birthday present. It is a Sky watcher's Cloud Chart. She noticed when they ran together that he always used to look at the sky.

They lay on the frozen soccer fields, trying to differentiate the different types of clouds. Tiffany tells Pat that she needs him, more than anything.

Pat realizes that, of all the people, Tiffany understands him. She knows how messed up he is, what he's done, and how many pills he's on. Even knowing all that, she's still here in his arms. Nikki would never have done that, not even on her best days.

Pat kisses Tiffany's forehead and tells her he needs her too.

Printed in Great Britain
by Amazon.co.uk, Ltd.,
Marston Gate.